Lord Shaftesbury

By

Laurie Sheehan

First published in 2001
by Anglia Young Books
Anglia Young Books is an imprint of
MILL Publishing
PO Box 55
4 Balloo Avenue
Bangor
Co. Down BT19 7PJ

Illustrations by Robin Lawrie

British Library Cataloguing-in-Publication Data

A catalogue record for this book is available from the British Library

ISBN 1 871173 69 8

Printed in Great Britain by
Ashford Colour Press, Gosport, Hampshire

Lord Shaftesbury

Author's Note

'No man has ever done more to lessen the extent of human misery or to add to the sum total of human happiness.'

Georgina Battiscombe,
Shaftesbury, A Biography of the Seventh Earl, 1801-1885, Constable, 1974.

During Lord Shaftesbury's 41-year Presidency of the Ragged School Union, the organisation enabled 300,000 destitute children to be educated free.

There have been many books on Shaftesbury since Edwin Hodder's *Life* (1886). I am particularly indebted to the works of

J.L. & Barbara Hammond,
G.F.A. Best,
Geoffrey B.A.M. Finlayson,
John Pollock,
Marion Bailey
and, of course,
Georgina Battiscombe.

Shaftesbury's life has been so well recorded that we know what he said. In just a few cases, to enliven the narrative, I have imagined what he may have said.

Chapter One

Although he lived in a grand house in London, Anthony Ashley-Cooper had a miserable childhood. His father bullied him and his mother hardly noticed him.

Only Maria, the housekeeper, was his friend. She was a deeply Christian woman who gave Anthony the love he never received from his family. He, in turn, adored her and, even though she died when he was eight, her influence stayed with him and he never forgot her kindness. She left him her gold watch, which he always wore.

Anthony was sent to boarding-school when he was seven, where he endured more bullying and more beating. Only Maria's letters to him kept him going. Then, when the boy was ten, his father inherited the title of the Earl of Shaftesbury, so Anthony, as the eldest son, became Lord Ashley.

When Ashley was twelve he went to Harrow School where, at last, he started to enjoy life. He grew tall and athletic, particularly enjoying boxing. He thrived at Harrow, and it was here, when he was fourteen, that something happened which was to shape his life.

He was walking alone down Harrow Hill one afternoon when he heard drunken laughter and yelling. Five men staggered from a side street, carrying a rough 'pauper's' coffin. One man stumbled and then the others fell over, too. The coffin hit the cobbles and the lid flew off. Out tumbled the body of an old man. The men swore and cursed and laughed at the corpse.

Ashley was horrified. 'Just because he was a poor, friendless old man, they have no respect for him,' he muttered.

His thoughts, as they often did, turned to Maria and how she had taught him about God's love for all people, rich and poor, and he resolved then, as he looked down on the stiff, naked body of the old man, to become, as he put it, 'The Friend of the Friendless'.

Chapter Two

Now that Ashley's father was the Earl of Shaftesbury, he opened up St Giles's House, the ancestral home at Wimborne St Giles, in Dorset.

Ashley loved going down there. 'For me, Dorset is a paradise compared with noisy, stinking London. Especially when Father's not here!'

But as he rode round the estate, he was shocked by the living conditions of the farm labourers. 'Such small cottages! So damp, cold, draughty, smelly and filthy! So many folk stuffed together.'

Ashley knew that his father wanted him to join the Army, but the boy hated the thought of a military career. He had other ideas; he wanted to change the world, to make life better for the common people. He wanted to have influence and, for this, he would have to enter Parliament, but first he was determined to get a university degree.

Fortunately, a family friend persuaded Ashley's father to let the lad study so, when Ashley was seventeen, he went to Oxford University.

As a 'tuft', a titled undergraduate, Ashley could have spent his time partying, but he was serious about his ambitions and he worked hard. For three years, he studied late by candle-light. He was very nervous before his Finals, and afterwards dreaded the result. But when it came: 'God be praised! a first!'

By now, Ashley was tall and handsome with long, curly black hair, hooded light-blue eyes and full red lips. Women loved him, not just for his looks but for his intelligence and his thoughtfulness. And he loved them, too!

Ashley's father had given him money for a two-year Grand Tour of Europe. 'Probably thinking, "the longer you stay away from me, the better!", said Ashley. So, in August 1823, he and an Oxford friend set off from Tower Stairs on the Thames aboard one of the new steam-powered boats.

A year later, in Vienna, Ashley fell in love with the beautiful Antoinette von Leykham. He wanted to marry her, but he knew it could not be. She was Roman Catholic; he was Church of England. If he married her, he'd cause himself many problems and forfeit any possibility of a life in politics. Later, he wrote sadly, in his diary: 'She was an angel, but she was surrounded by, and would have brought with her, a halo of hell.'

It was a sad return to England in August 1825. Not only did Ashley feel wretched about Antoinette, but his young brother, Francis, had been killed in a fight at Eton College.

His thoughts turned again to Maria and her gentle teaching. 'I won't feel sorry for myself,' he vowed. 'I have been put on this earth in comfortable circumstances so I can be "The Friend of the Friendless". It's time I began!'

So begin he did. He was elected Tory MP for Woodstock, Oxfordshire, but he found the cut and thrust of Parliamentary life hard to take. It depressed him and gave him stomach pains. 'I'm too bilious for public life,' he said. 'I'm not fit for the House of Commons.

But he persevered and became a member of a Select Committee on lunacy. One day he visited the dreaded White House, Bethnal Green, the largest privately owned pauper madhouse.

Long before reaching it, Ashley heard screams, roars and bangs and when he went inside, he was horrified at what he saw. Skinny, naked paupers lying in straw-filled wooden boxes. Men, women and children were wriggling in their own filth, struggling

to be free of the chains.

This visit affected Ashley deeply and he fought hard to change the lunacy laws. In February 1828, he made his first speech in Parliament and then helped frame the County Asylum Bill and the Madhouse Bill. The Bills became law, county asylums were built and inmates at last had some protection because the asylums were regularly inspected. Ashley himself was one of these inspectors.

Chapter Three

Ashley's beautiful Antoinette had married an Austrian prince in 1827, but she had died in childbirth. Ashley grieved for her and remembered their happy times together. He thought he would never know such love again.

But he was wrong! In the summer of 1829 he fell in love with Lady Emily 'Minny' Cowper. She was eighteen and regarded as the most beautiful girl in town. But Minny had already rejected four suitors and was in no rush to marry. It did not help that their two families disapproved of each other. Minny's family were fun-loving, free-thinking Whigs and Ashley's family were strait-laced Tories.

To Ashley's fury, Minny turned him down twice, but at last she accepted him and they were married at St George's, Hanover Square, on June 10 1830. Ashley's father had found an excuse not to come to the church but he did attend the reception and Minny soon charmed her crabby old father-in-law.

Not long after this the Tory Prime Minister, the Duke of Wellington, resigned and the Whigs came to power. Ashley rejected an offer to serve as a Minister with the Whigs, so he no longer had a Government salary. As the son and heir of a peer, he was not allowed to earn a living except in the Government or the Army. All he had was his father's small allowance and some help from Minny's family.

But the young couple were blissfully

happy, despite being poor compared with their friends, and in June 1831, baby Anthony was born. Ashley was determined to make his son's childhood as happy as possible. 'How can I fail,' he said, 'with my loving, calming, steadfast wife beside me?'

But other children were not so lucky. Ashley was back in Parliament, as MP for Dorsetshire, when, in February 1833, a Yorkshire clergyman, George Bull, came to see him. Bull had been sent to London by a committee representing Lancashire and Yorkshire factory hands. They were demanding that children work for no more than ten hours a day.

'They're slaves,' said Bull. 'Many die young, or are crippled and they are beaten by cruel overseers. In busy times, eight-year-old girls are working from three in the morning to half-past ten at night! And most receive no education. Please, Lord Ashley, will you put the cry of the children before Parliament?'

Ashley knew this would not be a popular campaign; he would make enemies of important people who wanted cheap labour. As Bull left, Ashley looked at Maria's watch. Then he asked Minny's advice.

Minny replied instantly, 'You've received a call from God that you dare not disobey. It is your duty to God and the poor. Go forward, and to victory!'

From that moment, Ashley thought of himself as 'The Children's Friend', too. He made a fine speech to a society for improving factory children's conditions. 'If this terrible system is permitted to continue any longer, the guilt will descend upon the whole nation. If the House will not adopt the Ten Hours Bill, they must drive me from the place, as I will not concede a single step.'

Minny gave birth to another boy, Francis, but Ashley's happiness was soured because Parliament had delayed his Ten Hours Bill. A Royal Commission had been appointed to report on factory conditions, because the mill owners wanted one.

But then the factory children themselves took action. On a hot June day in Bradford, a mob of them surrounded a team of Commissioners in a cobbled street. Barefoot and in smocks, the thin, pale-faced children had limped or staggered from their wool-spinning mill for a midday break. Many were deformed and all were weary but they still found the strength to sing:

'We will have the Ten Hours Bill,
That we will, that we will,
Or the land shall ne'er be still,
Ne'er be still, ne'er be still.
Parliament say what they will
We will have the Ten Hours Bill!
We want no Commissioning,
WE WILL HAVE THE TEN HOURS BILL!'

The Commissioners fled to the mill yard but were mobbed again. They were only rescued when the hooter called the children back to work.

Eventually, the Government replaced Ashley's Bill by one of their own and the Factory Act was passed. Children under nine

were banned from all mills except the silk mills. Those under thirteen must only work nine hours a day, ten hours in silk mills. Thirteen to eighteen-year-olds were limited to twelve hours a day and children would do no more night work; and all children between nine and thirteen must go to school for two hours daily.

Ashley thought, 'We haven't yet gained the "Ten Hours" for the older ones and the women, but at least we've helped the younger boys and girls a little.'

Chapter Four

By August 1839, Ashley needed a break. As well as worrying about the country's children, he now had six of his own! The whole family went to Birmingham on the new railway, then, leaving the five younger children with his sister Charlotte, he and Minny continued northwards to Liverpool, with the eight-year-old Anthony (Accy) and his nanny.

On arriving in the great port, they went for a stroll along the broad streets lined by splendid buildings. So much wealth! But behind the grand buildings were stinking alleys where the families of the Irish immigrants and the dock workers lived in filthy, crowded conditions.

The railway didn't go past Preston yet, so the family continued to the Lake District and to Scotland by horse and carriage. But Ashley couldn't ignore the conditions of the poor, wherever he went.

In the Highlands, he saw a gang of reapers cutting corn and asked what they were paid. 'One shilling a day to you women, and fifteen pence to you men, for twelve hours at harvest time!' he exploded. 'This is considered sufficient? And just two buckets of water to drink between all of you, and nothing to eat while you're in the fields!'

In Glasgow they visited a calico-printing works and Ashley was horrified by the working conditions, and hours, of the children employed in printing a pattern on the cotton cloth.

They also visited a school for the blind.

Ashley was President of the Indigent Blind Visiting Society, in England. The society improved life for the blind poor, providing guides to take them to churches and classes, and money in bad times.

Leaving his family behind, Ashley went, with a friend, to the Glasgow slums. They slithered through stinking, slimy alleys crammed with houses, dunghills and human beings. 'Heavens!' gasped Ashley. 'Who lives here? His friend sighed: 'Factory hands no longer fit for work. Broken in health, and spirit, they go from bad to worse till they come here and sink down in this dark pit of misery.'

Back in London, there was great rejoicing at the wedding of Queen Victoria and Prince Albert, on 10 February 1840. Ashley and Minny were invited to the wedding, but in the midst of all the pomp and ceremony, Ashley's thoughts were still back in the slums. 'What a contrast between the lives of rich and poor in this country!'

Very early one April morning, from an

upstairs back window of his house in Upper Brook Street, Ashley saw a sooty chimney-sweep and an even sootier 'climbing boy'. The lad looked about seven. The blood mingled with the soot on his bony knees and elbows as he stooped under the weight of the rods and brushes.

Ashley watched as they entered a hovel below, then he rushed out after them. He flung open the flimsy door. On the rickety table was a bowl of strong brine. The stinging salty water was used to harden knees and elbows by rubbing them with a rag in front of a fire.

He screamed at the sweep: 'What do you mean by apprenticing a boy so young? You're a tyrant, sir!' The sweep sneered. 'He's ten; the law says boys of ten can sweep chimneys.'

Ashley vowed to help this boy and went to see Robert Steven, known as 'The Climbing Boys' Champion'.

Meanwhile, a new 'Climbing Boys' Bill' was going through Parliament, strongly supported by Ashley. No child could be apprenticed until the age of sixteen, and certainly not climb till twenty-one. But many householders continued to use climbing boys, preferring them to sweeps with sweeping-machines. The fight was not yet over.

It was, for one lad, though. Robert Steven had tracked down the father of the boy Ashley had seen that day in April. Steven told the father that if he took the boy away from the sweep, Ashley would arrange free education. And the father agreed.

Now Ashley turned his attention to conditions in the coal mines. In June 1842, he introduced his Mines Bill and spoke with passion: 'A half-naked woman or child, with a chain attached to the waist, dragging a coal-truck through suffocating passages, sometimes just eighteen inches high. A four-year-old "trapper" sitting alone and terrified in the dark for twelve hours, pulling a string to open and close a ventilation trap-door. A squalling baby guarding its father's food from rats! This in mines owned by noble lords and cultured gentlemen.'

The Mines Bill was passed on 6 August, despite opposition from mine-owners in the House of Lords. The Mines Act barred boys under ten, and all women and girls, from underground work. Queen Victoria congratulated Ashley in person.

Chapter Five

Ashley had long been worried about London's 'wastrel children' who lived in hovels or under archways and in barrels. In February 1843, he read a *Times* advertisement asking for volunteer teachers. They were needed at the Field Lane Ragged School.

On a dark Thursday evening, Ashley visited the school. He could hear the screaming, swearing and singing of bawdy songs by the abandoned children as he climbed the stairs of the tumbledown house. As he entered, he saw a pale young male teacher cowering behind his desk as books were hurled at him.

The boys laughed at Ashley, who was holding a handkerchief to his face because of the stench. One boy was about to throw a book at him, when the teacher found his voice: 'This is Lord Ashley,' he cried. 'A good friend to people like you.'

Ashley's commanding voice filled the room and the din stopped. He told them the story of Jesus - and they listened! Afterwards he was convinced that Ragged Schools were one of the best means of helping the 'wastrels' out of the gutter and to find faith. Just as Maria had taught him, so would the volunteers bring religion to those whom the Church of England did not allow into its schools.

But he knew that volunteers alone could not teach every poor child in the land. Even those covered by the Factory Act were receiving little education. Most other children of the poor were getting none.

At least Ashley could help London children. In 1844, volunteers formed a Ragged School Union and he accepted the Presidency and worked tirelessly for it. He entered the slums behind the grand houses. 'Perhaps the rich, clattering by in their carriages, would help me if they knew what misery lurks here.' With his shoes in stinking pools, he slithered along the slimy alleys. He became friends with the ignorant and depraved. He urged them to send their young to the Ragged Schools. Many went: first in hundreds, then thousands.

Ashley was never satisfied with his achievements; there was still much to do for the mentally ill.

On 6 June 1845, Ashley, as Chairman of the Lunacy Commission, introduced two Lunacy Bills. He told Parliament: 'Those who are in their relatives' care are often in the worst plight of all. Such as the Welsh girl, Mary Jones. Her mother has kept her shut up for fifteen years in a tiny loft over a forge. The window has been boarded up, so she has little air and no light. My Commissioners found her bent and crouching, producing shocking deformity.'

He anxiously awaited the passage of the Bills through the House of Lords, where his father sat. On 23 July, Ashley wrote, 'My father, as usual, taking the lead in hatred and resistance to anything of mine. God turn his heart and give prosperity to the Bills.'

Despite his father, the Bills were passed. Now, every county had to build an asylum. There were stricter safeguards against wrongful detention. All patients were to be treated humanely. For the first time ever, they were regarded as persons of unsound mind not social outcasts.

And still, after thirteen years, Ashley was fighting to get his Ten Hours Bill through. On 29 January 1846, he reintroduced the Bill, but two days later, he'd resigned from Parliament, over the unjust Corn Laws. They taxed foreign corn, causing high bread prices because bad home harvests meant that there wasn't enough corn to feed everyone.

So the Ten Hours Bill was taken over by John Fielden. Though he was a mill-owner, he cared about his workers, and the Ten Hours Bill eventually became an Act of Parliament in 1847.

Soon, Ashley was back in Parliament as MP for Bath.

1848 was Europe's 'Year of Revolutions', but largely because of Ashley and his friends' mission work in the slums, England did not have a revolution. However, Queen Victoria was alarmed and summoned Ashley to Osborne House on the Isle of Wight. 'What should we do,' she asked, 'in view of the state of affairs, to show interest in the working classes?'

Ashley suggested that Prince Albert should visit some slum dwellers and then attend the anniversary meeting of the Labourers' Friend Society, which Ashley had founded.

With just two policemen as guards, Ashley led Albert and some gentlemen into the infamous slum part of St Giles-in-the-

Fields in London. Here, the Prince was given a warm reception, visiting tenement after rickety tenement. All the men left with smiles on their faces but black slime and swarms of bugs and lice on their fine clothes. The very poor now knew that Victoria and Albert really cared about them and the young couple were loved in return.

Ashley's next idea was to send some of the street children to better lives in Australia. The children were carefully selected and specially trained. He went to the riverside to see off the first, rather anxious, well-scrubbed group. The boys wore new, rough suits, the girls coarse-linen frocks.

'I see you now, my dear children, probably for the last time. You're going to a land where much will depend upon yourselves as regards your future prosperity and success in life. The whole world is open to you.'

Ashley also started a scheme for helping adult criminals to break away from their thieving ways. In less than a year, three hundred had either gone abroad or entered different employments at home, having no need to return to crime.

Then Ashley and Minny had their own tragedy. Their gifted sixteen-year-old Francis had been taken seriously ill with pleurisy, an inflammation of the lining of the chest wall. He fought bravely for two weeks but died at Harrow on 31 May 1849.

But within a week of burying Francis, Ashley was busy with his Ragged School Union meetings. As he told Minny, 'Work of the Ragged kind recalls Francis's dear face so vividly, and his dear words of sympathy and approval. How could I please him more were he alive?'

In November 1850, Ashley chaired a meeting of Ragged School teachers in the Field Lane schoolroom. They were discussing what the boys might do next year at Prince Albert's Great Exhibition of arts and sciences. Thousands of foreigners would be in London. 'Why not make some of our boys into shoeblacks, to clean the foreigners' shoes?' suggested one teacher.

So twenty-five uniformed boys of the Shoeblack Brigade cleaned 101,000 pairs of shoes at the glittering Crystal Palace, specially built in Hyde Park. With Ashley's support, brigades were also formed in the provinces.

Cholera had killed more than 53,000 people throughout Britain, over 14,000 in London alone. Ashley was now trying to improve the poor's health by putting two 'Lodging-House Bills' through Parliament. He'd visited so many of those filthy hovels and he wanted them improved. Once, he'd seen twenty-seven adults, thirty-one children and several dogs in one room!

While the Bills were passing the Commons, Ashley's father died and on 2 June 1851, Ashley became the seventh Earl of Shaftesbury.

Chapter Six

Shaftesbury successfully saw the Lodging-House Bills through the Lords. One Act put lodging-houses under local authority control. It required these houses to be licensed and to be inspected by police and medical officers. The other let big local authorities build their own model lodging-houses, paid for by the rates.

Ashley had long been shocked by the housing on his late father's estate - and the condition of St Giles's House. 'But what can I do?' he wrote. 'I am half pauperized; the debts are endless; no money is payable for a whole year; and I am not a young man. Every sixpence I expend - and spend I must on many things - is borrowed!' The debt was well over £100,000. But he managed to borrow enough money to repair the church and build cottages, and a school, with two more planned. St Giles's House would have to wait. His people adored him, the children calling him 'Lord Shaffy'.

One day, while driving over to take the salute at a review, Ashley passed a hobbling old woman. 'Get into the carriage,' he said. She did. Minutes later, the troops presenting arms grinned. Lord Shaftesbury was sitting in full uniform beside the coachman, and the blushing old woman was waving like a queen from the place of honour behind.

Another time, approaching a cottage to see a small girl reported sick, he heard her mum shout, 'Hie thee to bed, Jane, get big Bible out. Here's Lord Shaftesbury a-coming.'

He found Jane in bed, looking suitably religious. The Bible was open on the bedclothes, upside down at the Book of Amos!

A Bible was open, too, when his gentle son Maurice died, in 1855, but Shaftesbury arrived too late to see it because twenty-year-old Maurice, an epileptic, had been living in Switzerland for his health.

Shaftesbury was so famous now among the poor that every night when he arrived home exhausted, they were at the door of his house. On a cold and windy winter's night, he found a skinny man shielding a frail, shivering girl of about four. 'Your Lordship,' said the man, coughing blood, 'this is my daughter. She's starving. I can't get work; I have a consumption. I don't want to put her into the workhouse. Can she go to the colonies, where there's fresh air?'

Shaftesbury yawned, 'You must both come in. I'll put her in Mr William Williams's Broad Street Refuge for Girls. Mrs Edmond, the matron, will be taking girls to Canada. I'm sorry that you two must part but we'll find her a good family.'

He'd saved that man's daughter but he couldn't save his own beloved daughter Mary. In September 1861, she died, aged nineteen, from a dreadful lung disease. Ashley was shattered.

In 1866, Shaftesbury became patron of Williams's society, which ran Ragged Schools as well as Refuges. Here, the children received religious instruction and were taught reading, writing and arithmetic. The boys also learnt shoemaking, tailoring and carpentry. The girls did washing, cooking and cleaning, and made their own clothes, and shirts for the boys.

Shaftesbury wanted to take in far more children, give training for jobs at home and abroad and expand the society's activities. He discussed ideas with Williams. 'The Navy and Merchant Service are having trouble manning ships. There are old ships in the yards. Why not fit them out, fill them with street children and train them for naval service and for trades? Street boys are proud of their independence; we mustn't destroy that free spirit; they must choose to come to us. We'll announce a St Valentine's Night "treat" at the Boys' Refuge. If we invite the rich and the Press to watch, we could get a flood of donations to pay for the fitting-out of a vessel.'

Outside the large schoolroom in Great Queen Street, it was a cold, wet night. Inside, one hundred and fifty ragged lads, some who'd never used a fork before, ate the supper of a lifetime. Roast beef followed by plum pudding! Afterwards Shaftesbury asked the boys whether they'd like to be placed on board a training ship. 'Yes!' they shouted. 'Do you think another two hundred street boys would say the same?' 'Yes!' they yelled again.

He obtained a fifty-gun sail-rigged frigate, HMS *Chichester* and the funds rolled in. 'God speed our next project,' he thought. The next project was a farm school to train boys for colonial life.

On his rides through the Dorset countryside, Shaftesbury had often seen children working in the fields with their parents. It had never failed to remind him that it was not like this in East Anglia and parts of the south Midlands. There, small, bent-backed children worked in field gangs under cruel gang-masters.

Thanks to him, a Children's Employment Commission had been set up and he'd got this to report on these gangs. When the report came out, in 1867, he made a passionate speech in the Lords. 'Hannah and Sarah Adams, eleven and thirteen, worked for six weeks at Peterborough. Their home was eight miles away, so they walked sixteen miles a day. Their hours of work were from eight to half-past five. They left home at five in the morning, arriving back at nine at night. A younger sister, Susan, six, had worked with them but her strength failed!'

Later that year, an Act was passed preventing gang labour by any child under eight. It banned the employment of any woman or child in a gang where men were employed. Gang-masters were to be licensed.

They could only employ women or girls if a licensed gang-mistress accompanied the gang.

Time flew past. Shaftesbury had opened his Farm School, at Bisley, Surrey, and now here he was in London just finishing another visit to the poor. Leaving the slums, he felt for Maria's watch to check the time.

Gone! Picked from his pocket! He must ask his friends the thieves to help find it!

Some nights later, there was a knock at his front door. Whoever had knocked had fled but on the step was a big, wriggling canvas bag. He and the butler opened it. A little urchin was inside, too terrified to speak. In his shaking hand was the watch and pinned to his smelly rags was a badly spelt note: Giv im wot e diservs. Shaftesbury's eyes twinkled. 'You are going to school!' he said.

In 1868, Lord Shaftesbury became the President of the Golden Lane Mission to Costermongers.

Life was hard for the costers. They sold fruit, vegetables and fish from barrows pulled by donkeys. The costers' old homes in the

City area had long since been buried under railway yards, so thousands of costers struggled to survive in tenements, with several families - and donkeys - in one room.

Shaftesbury loved them, often spending evenings in their rooms. He brought God's Word to these rough, cheerful, independent folk who never went to church, except for weddings. He helped them in arguments with the authorities. He even joined the Barrow and Donkey Club which helped costers save to buy their own barrows and donkeys. He bought a donkey and a barrow, had it decorated with his coat of arms and lent it to his 'brethren'. As Vice-President of the Royal Society for the Prevention of Cruelty to Animals, he began donkey inspections, giving prizes for the best-treated animal. The costers enrolled Shaftesbury as one of themselves.

In July 1871, Shaftesbury had found yet another abuse of children - in the brickfields. 'I first saw, at a distance, what appeared like eight or ten pillars of clay. On approaching, I found to my astonishment that these pillars were living beings. They were so like the ground on which they stood, their features were so indistinguishable, their dress so besoiled and covered with clay that, until I saw them move, I believed them to be the products of the earth. They were so scared at seeing anything not like themselves, that they ran screaming as though something satanic was approaching. I followed them to their work. I saw little children, three-parts naked, tottering under the weight of wet clay, some of it on their heads, and some on their shoulders. And little girls with large masses of wet, cold and dripping clay pressing on their abdomens. Moreover, the unhappy children were exposed to the most sudden changes of temperature. For, after carrying their burdens of wet clay, they had to endure the heat of the kiln, and to enter places where the heat was so fierce that I was not myself able to remain more than two or three minutes.'

Through Shaftesbury's efforts, children were banned from brickfield work.

In March 1872, Shaftesbury hosted a

tea for mission leaders from London's rough areas. He wanted to know the state of progress of their Christian work. One speaker was a young, bespectacled little Irishman, Thomas Barnardo, whom Shaftesbury had met before and had encouraged. Barnardo had opened a boys' home in Stepney in December 1870. 'I arrived in London six years ago without a friend and without a farthing, and now run the largest Ragged School in the capital,' he said excitedly. Then he continued, 'And I've found vast numbers of urchins sleeping out!'

Late that night, Barnardo took Shaftesbury to a secret 'lay', where they found about seventy sleeping children. Shaftesbury refrained from telling young Barnardo that this was nothing new. He, Ashley, had found 'vast numbers' years before when Tom was only a lad himself.

On 15 October 1872, Minny died. She'd worn herself out caring for their twenty-six-year-old daughter, Conty, and for Cecil, twenty-three, who'd finally beaten typhoid fever.

Shaftesbury was distraught. He was greatly comforted, though, by a letter of condolence from Queen Victoria, written in her own hand. She understood his loss, for her beloved Albert had died eleven years before.

Then, on 16 December, Conty died, too, from tuberculosis.

Shaftesbury's hair, which had stayed black into his seventies, turned grey.

But his faith kept him going and he redoubled his efforts to get justice for the climbing boys. His earlier Chimney Sweeps' Bills and Acts had either been defeated or had no effect. One elegant lady had scoffed: 'A chimney sweep, indeed, wanting education! What next?' Shaftesbury had exclaimed in the Lords that a woman like that 'would cut up a child for dog's meat or for making manure!'

In October 1872, he had written in his diary, 'Years of oppression and cruelty have rolled on and now a death has given me the power of one more appeal to the public through *The Times*.'

Christopher Drummond, aged seven,

had died climbing the flue of a fernery at Washington Hall, near Gateshead. But nothing resulted from Shaftesbury's appeal. 'How many more deaths will be needed?' he thought.

In 1875, George Brewster, aged eleven, died after swallowing soot in a Cambridgeshire asylum flue. At last Shaftesbury's voice was heard and an Act was passed that year making the laws stronger. Sweeps would have to be licensed. Anyone breaking the law would be barred. Most important of all, the police were ordered to enforce these laws. 'Yet another scandal ended!'

The climbing boys - and girls - stopped climbing at last.

He'd been fighting for the animals, too! He pressed for shorter hours for the costers' donkeys, and he was successful. At a donkey show, some of them wore placards: 'Does not work on Sundays'. At a Golden Lane Mission meeting afterwards, Lord Shaftesbury, as chairman, got up from his chair and put his arm round a donkey called Coster, which had

DEN LANE MI

just been presented to him. 'When I've passed away from this life,' he said, 'I desire to have no more said of me than that I've done my duty, as the poor donkey has done his, with patience and unmurmuring resignation.' As Coster was led from the stage, Shaftesbury said, 'I hope the reporters of the Press will state that the donkey having vacated the chair, his place was taken by Lord Shaftesbury.'

Despite his advancing years, Shaftesbury continued his work in the House of Lords. He was involved with countless charities - founder, president, vice-president or patron of many. He was forever chairing meetings and committees, and was still unpaid Chairman of the Lunacy Commission. He politely answered his huge correspondence himself, never being able to afford a secretary.

One evening, he arrived home late with a City Mission friend to find yet more people on the doorstep. His friend urged him to ignore them but Shaftesbury ignored *him* and invited them in. Later, he showed his friend a photo of an old lady and a smiling girl of about sixteen. 'You see this sweet girl! Well, one cold night, when only four years old, she was brought by a poor man to my door, cold and starving. I took her in, and next day placed her in a home. She was sent to Canada with a batch of friendless ones. This lady took her into her service, educated her, and has now adopted her as her daughter. Their grateful letters make me glad that I'm a living man.'

One day when Shaftesbury was very old, he was sitting in a chair on the lawn of a Scottish mansion, gazing over the Firth of Clyde to the hills. He was growing deaf; his eyes were weak. His voice was weaker, too, but still retained the warmth and tone which had made his speeches so effective. He turned to old George Burns, the mansion's owner. 'If I followed my own inclination,' he said, 'I'd sit in my armchair and take it easy for the rest of my life. But I dare not. I must work as long as life lasts.'

Back in London, in wide and bustling

Oxford Street, Shaftesbury saw a small girl afraid to cross because of the horses' hooves and the rattling carriages and carts. She looked up at several passers-by but shook her head. As he approached, she timidly asked, 'Please, sir, will you see me across?' He took her hand and they braved the traffic together.

The streets were lined with thousands of girls and boys, braving the rain, on the day of Lord Shaftesbury's funeral service in Westminster Abbey. All were wearing something black, even if only a ribbon or scrap of cloth. There were crossing-sweepers, flower girls, shoeblacks, the disabled and boys from industrial schools, and men and women from the factories. Two hundred charities and caring institutions which he had led or helped were represented. The band of the Twickenham Boys' Home (opened in 1878) carried a banner, 'Naked and ye clothed me.' The boys from Great Queen Street had a banner saying, 'I was a stranger and ye took me in.' Many children were in the packed Abbey, including boys from the *Chichester,* and the *Arethusa* which had entered service in 1874.

The rain had stopped and the funeral procession moved towards Westminster Bridge and the costers' band played 'Safe in the Arms of Jesus'. The small girl from Oxford Street was here, too, remembering Shaftesbury's words after he'd helped her across: 'You didn't know that I was Lord Shaftesbury, so why did you ask me to help you?' 'Because you have a kind face,' she'd replied, smiling.

Epilogue

Lord Shaftesbury had died, on 1 October 1885, of an inflammation of the lung. He was 84. He was laid to rest in the family vault in the Church of Wimborne St Giles beside Minny, Mary and Conty.

The Ragged School Union is now called the Shaftesbury Society. This national Christian charity helps children and adults with learning and physical difficulties. It runs special schools and colleges, and provides supported-living and residential services for adults. Also, working with others, it helps poor families, the homeless, the unemployed and refugees.

Shaftesbury Homes and Arethusa is a separate society, originating from William Williams's Ragged Schools and Refuges. It continues his and Shaftesbury's work in a modern way. It runs homes in London's Wandsworth and Lambeth for children in care and has houses for the young homeless in London and Suffolk. At Lower Upnor, Kent, are the *Arethusa* sail-training ketch and the Arethusa Venture Centre.

PLACES TO VISIT

Websites:

www.shaftesburysoc.org.uk

and

www.shaftesbury.org.uk

Harrow School, Harrow-on-the-Hill, Middlesex

Old Schoolroom (prior application).

Bill Yard: coffin-incident plaque

'Eros' (Shaftesbury Memorial) Piccadilly Circus, London

Quarry Bank Mill, Styal, Wilmslow, Cheshire

18th-century working cotton mill.

Apprentice house, cottages, etc.

Armley Mills, Canal Road, Armley, Leeds

Formerly one of the world's largest woollen mills

Bradford Industrial Museum, Moorside Mills, Moorside Road, Bradford

Former wool-spinning mill re-created. Machines and working engines

Museum of Science and Industry In Manchester, Liverpool Road, Castlefield

Cotton machinery, mill engines, sanitary history: sewer - smells!

Helmshore Textile Museums, Holcombe Road, Helmshore, Lancashire

Working woollen fulling-mill and cotton-spinning mill

National Coal Mining Museum, Caphouse Colliery, Overton, West Yorkshire

Descend the 450 ft shaft!
Machinery and models

Big Pit Mining Museum, Blaenavon, Gwent

Descend the 300 ft shaft!
Miner's cottage.
Exhibits in pit-head baths

Cherished Chimneys, Station St, Longport, Burslem, Staffordshire

Climbing boy and chimney-pot museum: memorabilia, tapes